Be More VEGAN

NIKI WEBSTER

WELBECK

Published in 2021 by Welbeck Children's Limited,
part of Welbeck Publishing Group
20 Mortimer Street, London W1T 3JW

ISBN 978 1 78312 661 3

Printed in Dubai

10 9 8 7 6 5 4 3

Author, photographer and food stylist: Niki Webster
Illustrators: Anna Stiles, Emily Clarke
Nutritional consultant: Jessica English, Registered Dietitian
Design Manager: Emily Clarke
Designers: Darren Jordan, Matt Drew
Editor: Joff Brown
Production: Gary Hayes

WELBECK

Be More
VEGAN

NIKI WEBSTER

"We are the music makers,
And we are the dreamers of dreams."
Ode, Arthur O'Shaughnessy

Contents

Why am I VEGAN?

I was one of those weird kids (apparently) who didn't like meat and just refused to eat it. I didn't like the taste and the thought of eating animals felt wrong.

My poor mother didn't know what to do, especially when I developed a milk intolerance when I was seven. Back then there weren't the fantastic vegan options there are now, but we made do with what was around.

I was still labeled a fussy eater and I suppose I was, as I was eating quite a limited diet. But as soon as I could get in the kitchen as a teenager, I started cooking for myself, experimenting and discovering food that I loved to eat.

I've been cooking ever since, and I love how varied and exciting a plant-based diet can be. If like many people today, you're considering a vegan lifestyle, then it's important to stay healthy and eat well, so this book is packed with nutritional advice and delicious recipes that are good for you!

Remember, nobody's perfect and you don't need to be completely vegan to make a change, but if you're thinking about it, why not start by trying out some of my easy vegan favorites? Good luck!

Niki x

You don't need to become completely vegan overnight! But if you are thinking about it, you might need a bit of help, and some of the tasty recipes in this book...

PART ONE

Why be VEGAN?

WHAT IS VEGANISM?

When I first started eating and cooking vegan food, I was pretty unusual. Although there were lots of high-profile vegetarians out there, veganism and plant-based eating wasn't such a big thing. In recent years, however, more and more people are becoming vegan or talking about it —so what's it all about?

Veganism is a lifestyle that doesn't use anything that comes from an animal. This means not eating any kind of meat, but also eggs, milk, and any other dairy products. All vegan food is "plant-based," meaning it comes only from plants. Vegans also stay away from clothes, cosmetics, and household products made from animals.

It can sound a bit daunting! How do you know what's in the food you eat? Do you have to exist on lentils? What about when you're eating with family or friends? Is it okay to wear leather shoes? And what happens if you slip up and "accidentally" eat a Big Mac?

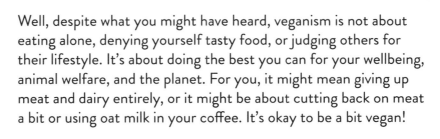

Well, despite what you might have heard, veganism is not about eating alone, denying yourself tasty food, or judging others for their lifestyle. It's about doing the best you can for your wellbeing, animal welfare, and the planet. For you, it might mean giving up meat and dairy entirely, or it might be about cutting back on meat a bit or using oat milk in your coffee. It's okay to be a bit vegan!

Remember—in today's world, it's unlikely that you're ever going to be "100% vegan." In our everyday life, many household products and everyday objects have been made with animal products. But every bit helps! Vegans are challenging companies to act more ethically all the time. And you can make a difference just eating more plant-based meals and sticking to cruelty-free products. The more people go plant-based, the more companies will decide to make products aimed at them.

You don't have to go it alone, either. These days, there are more vegan options in supermarkets, restaurants, and cafés than ever before. And it's only going to get better. Why not get your family involved? Even making a little change—say, having a meat-free family meal once a week—can make a big difference. And you get to try food that's bursting with flavor, like the recipes in this book.

So don't worry if you've never cooked a meal before, or you're still wearing those old leather shoes: being vegan is a fabulous journey, not a destination. And the more you change, the more the world will change with you. Being vegan—or even just making your diet a bit more plant-based—has never been easier or more fun!

ANIMAL WELFARE AND MORE

Animal welfare is at the heart of what it means to be vegan.

Being vegan is not just about what you eat, it's about a lifestyle that seeks to avoid cruelty to animals, while also looking for new ways to eat and live in a way that is sustainable to us and our environment. The Vegan Society, which was established in the UK in 1944, was the first to use the term "vegan" to describe a type of non-dairy vegetarianism.

"Veganism is a way of living which seeks to exclude, as far as is possible and practicable, all forms of exploitation of, and cruelty to, animals for food, clothing or any other purpose, and by extension, promotes the development and use of animal-free alternatives for the benefit of humans, animals and the environment."

www.vegansociety.com

The belief that animals have rights and should be treated with respect is not a new one, and although being vegan is quite recent, the practice of plant-based eating is much, much older!

The philosopher and mathematician Pythagoras, who lived in Ancient Greece and died in about 500 BCE, followed a vegan diet of raw food, because he and his many followers believed that all living beings have souls, so therefore it would be wrong to eat

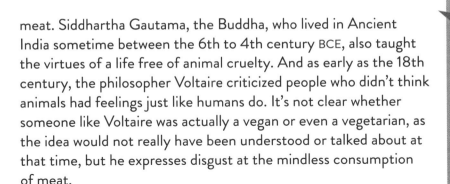

meat. Siddhartha Gautama, the Buddha, who lived in Ancient India sometime between the 6th to 4th century BCE, also taught the virtues of a life free of animal cruelty. And as early as the 18th century, the philosopher Voltaire criticized people who didn't think animals had feelings just like humans do. It's not clear whether someone like Voltaire was actually a vegan or even a vegetarian, as the idea would not really have been understood or talked about at that time, but he expresses disgust at the mindless consumption of meat.

> **"How pitiful, and what poverty of mind, to have said that the animals are machines deprived of understanding and feeling..."**
>
> Voltaire, *Philosophical Dictionary*, 1764

Like these early thinkers, many vegans and vegetarians today have made the decision not to eat meat, because they believe that the lives of animals are just as important as our own and that consuming any animal or meat product is therefore wrong. There are many associations and groups of activists who campaign actively for animal rights and believe that animals should never be exploited for experimentation, food, clothing, entertainment, or any other reason.

Some other people believe that it's okay to eat meat as long as farming, fishing, or hunting practices are not cruel to animals, so they choose only organically reared and free range produce, or opt for a diet which includes fish and other seafood.

SAVING THE PLANET

A plant-based diet can make a difference to the environment. So how much is too much meat?

According to a 2020 study from the Organisation for Economic Cooperation and Development, the world consumes over 347 million tons of meat per year. That's the equivalent of 50 times the weight of the Great Pyramid of Giza in Egypt. And if rates of meat consumption increase at the same rate, the world will be eating 500 million tons of meat per year by 2031—that's 71 pyramids!

All that meat-eating takes up a lot of land, a lot of water, and produces a lot of greenhouse gas emissions, so many people believe that if more of us adopt a vegan diet—or even reduce our meat consumption—we will be better able to tackle some of the world's environmental challenges.

The mass production of meat is only possible by using methods of industrial farming, which are not only cruel to animals, but are also tough on the environment.

But haven't humans always reared livestock and eaten meat? That's true, but in the last 100 years, the production of meat has sped up at what seems an alarming pace. According to a 2015 *Fortune* magazine article, in 1925 it took 112 days to raise a chicken that weighed 2.6 pounds, but now it takes only 48 days to produce a chicken that weighs in at a whopping 6.2 pounds. That's more than twice the meat in less than half the time, but at what cost?

The mass production of meat is cruel to animals, and it's destructive to the environment. Industrial farming uses large amounts of water, leading to deforestation and pollution and creating greenhouse gases, which contribute to global warming. What began with intensive chicken farming led to factory-scale pig rearing, and now beef cattle are also farmed on an industrial level in many places around the world.

It's difficult to accurately measure how much environmental damage meat production causes, especially as it relies on growing grain and soy crops in order to feed livestock, and these practices also have an impact.

The world's meat consumption per year: 50 times the weight of Egypt's Great Pyramid of Giza!

According to a study by the World Wildlife Fund, around one-third of the world's grain production is fed to livestock, and almost the same amount of the earth's land surface is used for meat production—so just imagine what else we could do with those valuable resources if we didn't eat so much meat!

VEGAN FASHION

If being vegan is about more than just what you eat, how can you avoid other things which might have caused harm or suffering to animals? How can you make sure that the choices you make about what to wear and what to buy make sense for a vegan lifestyle?

CLOTHING AND ACCESSORIES

Vegans believe that they shouldn't wear leather or fur, as animals were killed for these products. Some also avoid any product which has come from an animal, so would not buy silk, which is made by silkworms. (Silkworms are a type of caterpillar, which produce silk inside their cocoons—they are killed so that the silk strands can be extracted.)

Although sheep are not killed to get wool, the process of shearing can be uncomfortable or even cruel if performed by shearers concerned with efficiency over animal welfare. So wool is often avoided by strict vegans too.

Although there are many clothes and accessories which are not made of animal products, it's not always easy to spot whether fabrics or clothes have been colored with dye tested on animals. If you're really serious about making a positive impact on animal welfare and the environment, you can always check the labels to find out how and where clothes were manufactured. If clothing is ethically sourced, you can usually find this on the label.

Top Tip

There are now plenty of great vegan fashion brands available using "pleather" instead of leather for shoes, bags, and other items. Some good choices for clothing are fair trade cotton, linen, or bamboo.

COSMETICS AND SKIN CARE

Lots of makeup, hair, and body products are not vegan, as they contain ingredients which have come from animals. If you want to avoid animal-based products then check the labels for any of these: lanolin (from sheep's wool); shellac (from lac bugs); glycerine (from animal fats); collagen (from cows or marine animals); elastin (from muscles, ligaments, and aortas of animals); and keratin (from feathers, horns, or wool).

As well as including animal ingredients, many cosmetics are tested on animals to ensure they are safe for human use. These tests can cause pain and suffering to animals, so if you want to find cosmetics that are produced without animal testing, then check out the labels and look for products that are marked "cruelty-free" or "suitable for vegans."

IN YOUR HOME

It's almost impossible to be completely vegan in your home, as so many things have hidden animal products within them like glue or dye.

Feathers and down are common fillings for cushions, pillows, and duvets, so you may decide you want to avoid these. Luckily, there are plenty of synthetic or non-animal versions available, so make sure you check out the manufacturing label before you buy!

Whatever you decide, it's never a bad idea to read the labels or the product information before you choose what to buy—as well as cruelty-free information, you can usually find out lots about your product just by reading the fine print.

THE AWKWARD QUESTIONS...

Here are the most common questions I've had about veganism over the years ... and my answers!

Q "Do you only eat lettuce?"

A The classic question—definitely not in my case and I hope this book will help you with some recipe ideas and inspiration. No limp lettuce in sight!

Q "What is nutritional yeast— is it the bread yeast you get in the little tubs or sachets?"

A A common mistake, and I get asked it all the time. Nutritional yeast is de-activated yeast, very different from bread yeast. It has a nutty, savory taste and is used to give a cheesy flavor to vegan dishes.

Q "Will I be lacking in protein? Especially if I do a lot of exercise?"

A As long as you're eating enough food to support your growth and health, it's very unlikely that you'll be lacking in protein. Eating a wide variety of plant-based food throughout the day will enable your body to make complete proteins.

Q "Aren't you going to be deficient in vitamins and minerals if you don't eat meat?"

A You can get what you need from a balanced plant-based diet, as the key nutrients you need are also found in plants. Vitamin B12 is the exception (see below). In my opinion, you can also be deficient if you eat an unbalanced meat-based diet. However, it's important to eat mindfully to ensure you get what you need.

Q "Can you get enough vitamin B12?"

A Many products now have added vitamin B12, including fortified plant milks and breakfast cereals. Always check the label on your plant milk to make sure it includes vitamin B12. Speak to your doctor who can advise you on whether you'll need a supplement.

Honey

Q "Is honey vegan?"

A Honey isn't vegan as it's produced by the labor of bees. However, some people following a "plant-based" diet eat honey.

Q "Is soy bad for the environment?"

A Soy is a fantastic source of plant-based protein but is also a main cause of rainforest deforestation. However around 80% of the world's soy is fed directly to livestock and only 6% is turned into human food.

Q "But you can't be 100% vegan, can you?"

A The short answer to that is probably not—as animals or animal derivatives are used in manufacturing processes and it's almost impossible to check the label on everything you consume (plus sometimes it's hard to understand the terminology). However, you can make a conscious choice to choose a vegan diet and make ethical purchase decisions— that goes a long way.

Q "Is veganism just a fad?"

A In my opinion, it's not. More and more people are thinking about their own personal impact on the environment, and finding ways to minimize that impact. Veganism and plant-based eating have gained such momentum over the last few years—it's hard to imagine that the movement will diminish.

Q "Can you use plant-based milk for hot drinks?"

A There are so many amazing plant-based milks around now. The new creamy "barista" style milks are perfect for hot drinks.

PLANT-BASED CONUNDRUMS

So if you want to help the environment, how can you be sure that vegan food is not harmful too?

The main thing is to think about the food you eat, how it was produced, where it comes from, and how it got to you. So for example, if you choose to eat plant-based convenience foods you will certainly be avoiding the harmful impact of processed meat, but it may be that the ingredients have been shipped across the world to get to you, and may come in non-recyclable packaging. Your ready-meal might be healthy, but it might also have a large carbon footprint!

Likewise, soy is a fantastic source of plant-based protein and is a key ingredient in many vegan dishes, yet the production of soy is one of the main causes of rainforest deforestation. Some might argue that soy is therefore a poor environmental choice for vegans, but according to a 2017 World Wildlife Fund report, 80% of the world's soy is fed directly to livestock. Only 6% is turned into human food. The picture isn't always straightforward!

Another product responsible for widespread deforestation of rainforests is palm oil, which is used in a range of convenience foods, including many vegan cakes and spreads. Palm oil is also contained in a number of common household products, so make sure you check the labels if you are out shopping—and always look out for sustainable and ethically sourced ingredients.

And what about foods like avocados and quinoa, which have lots of health benefits and are popular choices for many vegetarians and vegans?

Well, avocados contain lots of healthy fats, but the increase in demand for avocados has put a lot of strain on farmers and has led to forests being thinned for avocado plantations. This kind of intensive farming contributes to greenhouse emissions. Plus, of course, if your avocado is coming from across the world, then it's racking up the food miles, so that also has an impact!

Eating right feels like a minefield and it's easy to get confused, but if you can try to source natural, fresh, and local ingredients and cook with them, that's a good start.

The environmental and social impact of quinoa is just as confusing. This traditional, nutrient-rich grain has grown so much in popularity that local producers in the Andean region of South America are now getting three times the price for their produce. Great news, right? Well maybe not. According to a 2015 North American Congress on Latin America report, quinoa is now so expensive that the local population is turning away from this traditional staple, and eating a poorer and cheaper diet.

So remember: it's not always possible or practical to make "perfect" choices—but making mindful choices is a good way to approach it!

PART TWO

Be vegan, be HEALTHY!

HOW TO STAY HEALTHY

I'm passionate about food and cooking and I believe that being vegan is one of the healthiest—and most delicious—ways to eat!

However, some people worry that a purely plant-based diet won't provide all the nutrients and protein that a young person needs, especially if they're still growing, or leading an active lifestyle. So it's important to be mindful of your food choices and responsible about nutrition—try to eat a balanced, varied diet packed full of fresh vegetables, fruit, pulses, grains, and nuts.

In this section I'll look at the nutritional requirements needed to achieve a healthy vegan diet. You'll see that a well-planned, balanced vegan diet usually contains more fresh fruit and vegetables than other ways of eating, as well as more whole grains, beans, lentils, nuts, and seeds. This means that vegans often eat comparatively more fiber and less saturated fat than non-vegans, which has been linked to better heart health, as well as reducing the risks of type two diabetes and some forms of cancer.

In thinking about the recipes for this book, my focus has been on creating varied, healthy, but fun dishes, which include lots of fresh vegetables, fruit, pulses, grains, nuts, and seeds. They have been checked by a dietitian to ensure they will provide many of the nutrients you need as part of a balanced vegan diet. But like all recipes, they need a little planning and know-how to make sure you have all the ingredients. Think ahead and plan your week's menu, so you don't end up eating the same thing all the time.

If in doubt, you could try introducing plant-based meals into your normal diet, one or two times a week, to see how it works for you!

IS ALL VEGAN FOOD GOOD FOR ME?

Don't forget, not all vegan food is healthy—you could easily have an unhealthy vegan diet (like any diet).

The health benefits of veganism come from eating fresh vegetables, fruit, whole grains, pulses, nuts, and seeds which are rich in nutrients and fiber. French fries are usually vegan, but if you only ate those, it would be very unhealthy!

THE PERFECT BALANCE

It's not possible to have a "perfect" diet all the time—and this book includes some tasty treats for special occasions—but if you follow the guidelines here, this should give you an idea of what to include to keep healthy.

HERE'S HOW THE U.S. DEPARTMENT OF AGRICULTURE SAYS YOU SHOULD DIVIDE UP YOUR DIET.

Fruit & vegetables
Fruit and vegetables should make up the largest percentage of your food. Eat as many different colors as you can. Canned and frozen fruit and veggies count too!

Tofu, beans, nuts, seeds, and soya-based foods like veggie sausages or mince. Pulses and legumes (plants that are related to pulses) count too—it doesn't matter if they're fresh, canned, or dried.

Protein-rich foods

DON'T FORGET

Choose unsaturated fats where you can

Stay hydrated, especially if you're eating more fiber than usual

Aim for at least 5 servings of fruit and vegetables every day

Look for protein-rich foods like nuts, seeds, pulses, and legumes

Include foods rich in calcium

Make sure you have sources of vitamin B12

Enjoy foods that are high in fat or sugar in smaller amounts

Go for the fortified versions of dairy alternatives, with added vitamins and minerals

Starchy carbohydrates

Carbs include bread and cereals, oats, rice, pasta, rice cakes, couscous, noodles, and potatoes. Despite what you might have heard, these should make up over a third of your food!

Oils & spreads

Calcium-rich foods

Unsaturated oils and spreads such as rapeseed oil and olive oil. Use in small amounts.

Vegans can get their calcium from fortified (non-organic) plant milks and yogurts. Calcium is also present in foods including cabbage, broccoli, and calcium-set tofu.

NUTRITION NEEDS

A healthy and balanced vegan diet should be able to provide you with what you need for good health—however, here are some of the key nutrients to be aware of when considering a vegan diet. The values shown are averages—everyone's intake will differ slightly.

VITAMIN B12

Boys & girls aged 11-14:	Boys & girls aged 15-18:
1.2 micrograms per day	1.5 micrograms per day

Vitamin B12 helps to make red blood cells, keeps a healthy heart and circulation, and helps prevent nerve damage. It is found in meat, fish, eggs, and dairy, but not in fruit or vegetables. Both vegans and meat-eaters can be deficient in B12. However, the condition is more prevalent in vegans and vegetarians.

There are no reliable plant-based sources of B12, and so it's recommended to eat fortified foods at least twice a day (aiming for 3 micrograms of B12 per day) or to take a supplement. If you're not eating fortified foods, you will definitely need to take a supplement. Speak to your doctor about the amounts you'll need.

GOOD SOURCES
Fortified foods: breakfast cereals, plant milks and yogurts, vegan spreads, some meat substitutes (check the label).

If you're concerned about your intake, you'll need to speak to your doctor. They may take a blood test to check your levels and refer you to a dietitian to discuss how to get enough from your diet.

IRON

Girls aged 11-18:	Boys aged 11-18:
14.8 milligrams per day	11.3 milligrams per day

Iron is essential for the proper function of haemoglobin, which helps to carry oxygen around your body. Iron is found in red meat, fish, and poultry, but also in many plant-based sources.

GOOD SOURCES
Pulses, legumes, dark green leafy vegetables, tofu, nuts, seeds, partially dried fruits. Try to include one source of iron per meal.

PROTEIN

Girls aged 15-18:	Boys aged 15-18:
Around 45 grams per day	Around 55 grams per day

Protein is essential for building muscle. Getting enough is rarely a problem, but some people are concerned about the amount of protein in a plant-based diet. You can create a complete plant-based protein by combining a variety of pulses and grains.

GOOD SOURCES
Tofu, beans and pulses, nuts, nut butters, quinoa.

CALCIUM

Girls aged 11-18:	Boys aged 11-18:
800 milligrams per day	1,000 milligrams per day

Calcium builds healthy teeth and bones, and is essential for the proper functioning of your heart, muscles, and nerves.

GOOD SOURCES
Whole grains, pulses, green leafy veggies and fortified plant milks.

OMEGA 3 FATTY ACIDS

Diets rich in omega 3 fatty acids may be helpful for protecting our heart health and memory.

Omega 3s are made up of two different types of fatty acid:

ALA—which our body can't make, so the only way we get any is through our diet.

EPA and **DHA**—fatty acids which can be made from the ALA building blocks in our bodies. These are thought to have the most health benefits.

The main source of EPA and DHA omega 3 fatty acids is oily fish, but our bodies can convert some plant-based sources of ALA into EPA and DHA after we've eaten them.

GOOD SOURCES
You can get some ALA from nuts and seeds, vegetable oils, some soya products like tofu and soya milk, and some green leafy vegetables. Some foods are also enriched with omega 3s.

ZINC

Helps our bodies to heal, build new cells, and process our food.

GOOD SOURCES
Whole grains, nuts, seeds, fermented food like tempeh and miso.

FORTIFIED FOODS

Some popular vegan foods are fortified with extra nutrients, especially vitamin B12 and calcium. This includes some plant milks and yogurts, some bread and juices, some meat substitutes, and some breakfast cereals. Check the label to ensure that they're fortified.

SELENIUM

Helps our immune and reproductive systems to work properly.

GOOD SOURCES

Nuts, grains, seeds. Two to four brazil nuts per day gives you your recommended daily allowance.

IODINE

Helps our thyroid to function, and supports a healthy metabolism.

GOOD SOURCES

Harder to get from plant-based sources, though it is increasingly being added to fortified plant milks and yogurts (check the label). Speak with your doctor if you're not eating any dairy or animal products and you're concerned you're not getting enough.

VITAMIN D

This vitamin works with calcium to help support healthy teeth, muscles, and bones. Our bodies make vitamin D when exposed to the sun. During the winter months, supplements may be needed to reach the recommended daily intake of 600 IU. Speak to your doctor before starting any supplements.

EAT MORE BEANS!

Pulses are the edible seeds inside legume pods, and include beans, peas, and chickpeas. They're categorized as both a protein and a vegetable, and they're one of the best things you can add to a vegan diet.

Beans are a great source of plant-based protein and have been a staple of many traditional cuisines and in vegan diets. They are nutrient-dense, rich in antioxidants, and contain heart-healthy fiber.

You can buy beans in cans or jars, but buying dried beans and soaking them is usually the cheapest option and it tastes better too. Always remember to follow soaking and cooking instructions, as some beans are poisonous until properly soaked and cooked. If you buy in cans, look for BPA-free and without sugar or salt.

DRIED PULSES SOAKING & COOKING CHART

DRIED BEANS	SOAKING TIME*	COOKING TIME*
Black beans	Soak overnight	1-1½ hours
Black-eyed beans	Soak overnight	30 mins - 1 hour
Butter beans	Soak overnight	40-50 mins
Cannellini beans	Soak overnight	45 mins - 1½ hours
Chickpeas	Soak overnight	1½ hours
Kidney beans	Soak overnight	1½-2 hours
Pinto beans	Soak overnight	1½-2 hours
Mung beans	Soak for 2 hours	25-40 mins
Red split lentils	No need to soak	15-20 mins
Green & brown lentils	No need to soak	35-45 mins
Puy lentils	No need to soak	25-35 mins
Yellow lentils	No need to soak	40-45 mins
Split peas	Soak for 2 hours	30-35 mins

*All values are approximate—timings may vary

PERFECT PULSES

There are hundreds of varieties of pulses—here's a few you should get to know...

BEANS

black-eyed, fava, kidney, butter, haricots, cannellini, flageolet, pinto, borlotti

Beans are great for boosting salads, chili, and soups.

LENTILS

red, green, yellow, and brown

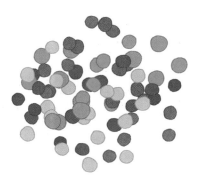

Ideal instead of ground beef, simple to cook, and tastier than you might think!

CHICKPEAS

channa and garbanzo beans

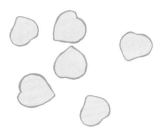

The main ingredient in hummus, and amazing in curries.

PEAS

garden, split

Easy to cook from frozen, peas add a pop of flavor to any dish.

PART THREE

The Vegan KITCHEN

VEGAN SUBSTITUTES

There's a huge selection of plant-based swaps for all your favorite foods out there—here are some of my favorites.

MILK

Milk is one of the easiest swaps as there are so many fantastic options to choose from and they're available almost everywhere— you can pick up everything from almond and oat to creamy coconut blends. It's easy to make your own, but the benefit of store-bought milk is that it's usually fortified with calcium and other hard-to-get nutrients. Try lots and see which ones you like best!

CREAM AND YOGURT

To add creaminess and richness in the place of cream or yogurt, coconut is a dream ingredient—it adds a huge amount of texture and flavor to vegan food, and a little goes a long way.

Coconut yogurt
Add a few tablespoons to curries, soups, and stews for a rich creamy texture and flavor. It's perfect for making creamy dips like raita, and delicious stirred into oats.

Coconut cream

This is the thick part at the top of a can of coconut milk, but you can also buy it separately. It's the key to deliciously creamy desserts like ganache, mousse, and cheesecake.

Coconut milk

Ideal for making creamy curries, rice, and desserts.

Silken tofu

When blended, this delicate tofu becomes smooth and creamy. Believe it or not, you can make a delicious mousse with silken tofu, chocolate, and a little coconut oil!

CHOCOLATE

It's very easy to find great dairy-free chocolate. Good quality dark chocolate is usually dairy-free anyway. Since chocolate is made from cocoa beans which are then dried and fermented, it's naturally vegan. It's only the process of adding milk which makes it non-vegan. Many chocolate makers now add coconut or plant-based milk instead of cow's milk, and there are lots of amazing dairy-free chocolate bars and truffles out there.

EGGS

Vegans have lots of options for replacing eggs. In baking it's really easy, as there are a variety of options to choose from to bind things together. The different alternatives are suitable for different baked goods. One of the most widely known is making a chia or flax "egg" —one tablespoon of flax or chia seeds, plus two tablespoons of water per "egg"—but here are some other clever swaps:

Aquafaba

Use 3 tablespoons of whipped chickpea water instead of one egg.

Banana
Mashed banana is an excellent binder and sweetener in desserts.

Avocado, chestnuts
These add moisture and bind well when blended into a paste.

Peanut butter
3 tablespoons per egg. Perfect for brownies!

Silken Tofu
To achieve an egg-like texture and flavor for scrambles and "omelettes," silken tofu works well. Add some black salt for a pretty convincing eggy taste. You can combine gram flour, tofu, nutritional yeast, and caramelized onions to make a plant-based omelette which you can add lots of toppings to.

PANTRY ESSENTIALS

I always have these ingredients on hand so I can whip up awesome vegan meals easily! Why not try buying one or two every time you shop, so you build up a good collection?

DRIED GOODS

Red split lentils—Packed with goodness, these easy-to-cook lentils are great for soups, dahls, and stews.

Puy lentils—The earthy flavor of these "meaty" lentils is amazing.

Quinoa—A complete plant-based protein.

Rice—White or brown rice goes with everything. Arborio rice makes amazing risottos.

FLOURS

Plain flour & wholemeal wheat flour—These are great for fluffy flatbread and pizza bases.

Buckwheat Flour & Gram Flour—My favorite gluten-free options.

Rye & Spelt—These "ancient grains" have a lovely nutty texture.

NUTS AND SEEDS

Seeds—Dry toast them to enhance the flavor.

Nuts—Essential for adding texture, protein, and good fats.

Nut butters—Peanut or almond butter makes the perfect healthy toast topper.

Tahini—Crushed sesame seeds, great for hummus and dressings.

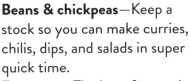

CANS

Beans & chickpeas—Keep a stock so you can make curries, chilis, dips, and salads in super quick time.

Tomatoes—The base for meals in minutes.

Coconut milk & coconut cream—For creamy curries and desserts.

OILS, SEASONING, SPICES AND HERBS

Olive oil—Use this for cooking and roasting.

Extra virgin olive oil—This has a stronger flavor, great for making dressing, drizzles, dips, and pestos.

Toasted sesame oil—For adding toasted flavor to Asian dishes.

Coconut oil—Works well for Asian food.

SEASONINGS

Salt/Sea Salt flakes

Black Pepper

Lemon juice—Immediately enhances flavor.

Vegetable Stock—Check the label, it's not always vegan.

SPICES

Indian spice—Cumin seeds, black mustard seeds, turmeric, coriander, garam masala.

Smoky flavors—Smoked paprika and ancho chilli.

Middle Eastern—Fennel, caraway.

Heat—Chili flakes, hot paprika, cayenne pepper.

Sweet—Cinnamon, ginger, allspice, mixed spice.

CONDIMENTS

Soy/Tamari **sriracha**—This powerful chili sauce boosts meals in seconds.
Rose harissa/harissa—Adds incredible depth of flavor and color.
Nutritional yeast—The magic ingredient for making anything taste nutty, cheesy, and creamy! With cashews, it makes the perfect cheese sauce, and it's a great source of B vitamins.

FRESH HERBS

Mint—For dips, salads, and desserts.
Coriander—Perfect for flavoring Asian dishes.
Basil—The "king of herbs". Essential for creating batches of pesto.
Spinach—A versatile leaf. Add it to salads, curries, pestos, and stews.
Thyme—Delicious in tomato dishes.

FRIDGE

Plant-based milks—There are some excellent plant-based milks in stores now, including **oat**, **almond**, **coconut**, **cashew**, and **soy**.
Cheese—Try store-bought or make your own (see page 38).
Tofu—Firm tofu is great for stir-fries.
Plant-based yogurt—Add to curries, soups, and stews for a rich creamy texture and flavor.
Vegan butter
Vegan mayo

FREEZER

Frozen veggies—Use frozen peas to make an amazing dip or mash in minutes, or try adding them to curries for fantastic plant-based protein.
Frozen peas
Corn
Edamame
Frozen fruit

KITCHEN CONFIDENCE

Whether you're a budding chef or a total novice in the kitchen, these tips will help get you cooking.

HOW TO PLAN YOUR RECIPE

The most important thing is to read the recipe first and check you have the ingredients and equipment needed. Then get the ingredients out and chop everything first. Before starting to cook, organize your equipment—this makes cooking much less stressful.

What if you don't have the exact ingredients?
- You can swap most vegetables and pulses.
- Most flours are interchangeable.
- Missing a spice? Try a new combination.

Staying Safe and Clean
- Make sure you always wash your hands before you start cooking.
- Pop on an apron to keep your clothes clean.
- Wash any fruit and vegetables before cooking.
- Make sure your cooking area is clean and you have a clean cloth handy.
- Collect any food waste in a bowl, ready to be composted.
- Be careful with hot ovens—always use oven mitts!
- A sharp knife is essential to chopping—but be careful and always protect your fingers.
- Never put your hands in food processors or blenders when they are switched on.

WEIGHTS & MEASUREMENTS
Spoon measurements
3 teaspoons = 1 tablespoon
16 tablespoons = 1 cup

Abbreviations
tsp = teaspoon
tbsp = tablespoon
oz = ounce

Watch out!
It's easy to get these confused!

INGREDIENTS

For almond or hazelnut milk

4 oz almonds or hazelnuts (soaked for at least 4 hours, or overnight)

4 cups filtered water

2 - 3 pitted medjool dates or 1 tsp maple syrup

Pinch of sea salt

For creamy cashew milk

4 oz cashews (soaked for at least 4 hrs, or overnight)

4 cups filtered water

1 tbsp maple syrup (optional)

1 tsp vanilla extract (optional)

Pinch of sea salt

Choc milk option

2 tbsp raw cacao powder

MAKE YOUR OWN PLANT MILK

Although it won't have the same nutritional content as fortified plant milks, making your own plant-based milk is fun and easy. Just grind up some nuts or seeds in a high-speed blender and, *voilà*, nut milk! To filter out all the bits, you can use a special nut milk bag—these are made with a fine mesh, and they're easy and cheap to buy online.

EQUIPMENT

High-speed blender
Nut milk bag
Glass bottles for storage

TO MAKE THE MILK

1. Drain and rinse the soaked nuts.

2. Add the ingredients for your chosen milk to the high-speed blender. If you want chocolate milk, add the cacao powder too!

3. Blend well for 30 seconds to 1 minute, until milk is smooth and creamy.

4. You can strain through a nut milk bag, gently pressing the bag so the milk runs out into a bowl. If you don't have a nut milk bag, just pour straight into glass bottles for storage in the fridge, if you don't mind the pulp in your milk making it a bit thicker.

1

2

3

4

37

Top Tip

The milk can be stored for up to 3 days in the fridge, or you can freeze it for up to 6 months.

NUT CHEESE CHALLENGE

You can find lots of vegan "cheese" options in stores, but why not try to make your own? It's easier than you think!

It's really easy to make a quick nut cheese using soaked cashews and some "cheesy" nutritional yeast. You can also use almonds or macadamia nuts, but cashews have the creamiest texture. Or you could try making fermented nut cheese. Instead of the cheesy flavor being added by the yeast, it's created by using a probiotic capsule to ferment the cashews. The fermented version will last up to three months in the fridge and will develop a stronger taste over time.

EQUIPMENT
High-speed blender—This is very important, so you get a very creamy texture.
Glass/wooden bowl & spoon—Don't use metal if fermenting, as it stops the fermentation process.
Ramekins
A clean cloth

TO MAKE THE CASHEW PARMESAN

Add all the ingredients to a food processor and blend briefly, but not too much as you want a crunchy, crumb-like texture.

TO MAKE UNFERMENTED CHEESE

Add all the ingredients to a food processor or high-speed blender and blend until smooth and very creamy. Ensure there are no lumps.

TO MAKE THE FERMENTED CHEESE

1. Drain and rinse the soaked cashews. Add the water and cashews to a food processor or high-speed blender, and blend until smooth and creamy.

2. Transfer to a large glass or wooden bowl. Add a pro-biotic capsule (open the plastic capsule and pour the contents in). Stir with a wooden spoon.

3. Cover with a clean cloth for 24 hours at room temperature.

4. After 24 hours, taste it to see if it has a slightly sour flavor. If it still tastes like cashews, cover and let sit for another day. Now season with salt and pepper and flavor as desired, then mix well.

5. Transfer to small pots or ramekins. Pop in the fridge, and keep for up to three months.

For the fermented cheese

8 oz cashews, soaked for at least 4 hours
Water to cover
1 probiotic capsule

Seasoning

1 tsp salt
Pinch of black pepper

Flavor options

1 tsp smoked paprika
1 tsp garlic powder
1 tsp cumin or fennel seeds

BREAKFAST

Rise and shine! Start your day with these fantastic plant-based morning meals.

Build-your-own oat cups

INGREDIENTS
Makes 2-4 cups

....

For the oats
2 cups oats
Plant-based milk to cover

TOPPINGS
Banana peanut butter
¼ banana, chopped
1 tsp nut butter

Bircher
½ grated apple
1 tsp nut butter
Pinch cinnamon
1 tbsp dried fruit

Blackberry compôte
150g blackberries
1 tsp maple syrup
Splash of water

Or why not try...
Plant-based yogurt
Fresh berries
Nuts & seeds
Maple syrup

This is the perfect ready-made breakfast!
You just need to soak a batch of oats on a Sunday night and then choose your tasty toppings on weekday mornings. Mix and match—the choice is yours...

TO MAKE THE OVERNIGHT OATS

1. Add the oats and plant-based milk to a large container—make sure the oats are well covered.
2. Secure a lid and place in the fridge overnight.
3. In the morning, remove and portion into a bowl.
4. Add one of the topping options, stir, and dig in!

TO MAKE THE TOPPINGS

1. For the banana peanut butter and bircher toppings, simply mix the ingredients into your oats.
2. For the blackberry compôte, add the ingredients to a saucepan and simmer on a low heat for around 5 minutes, until the mix has thickened slightly. Leave to cool and add to your oats.

Niki's tip
Try soaking the oats in individual cups the night before, for the ultimate healthy portable breakfast.

INGREDIENTS
Serves 8

Wet ingredients
3 ripe bananas, mashed
2 tbsp peanut butter
3 tbsp plant-based milk
2 tbsp maple syrup

Dry ingredients
1 cup oats
1 tsp baking powder
1 tsp cinnamon
4 tbsp ground almonds
2 tbsp sunflower seeds
1 cup berries—your choice

Toppings
A few more berries
Nuts
Seeds

Banana berry breakfast bars

These bars taste great, they're super easy to make, and you can add in any extra ingredients you have in the house. The bananas are the magic ingredient—they add natural sweetness and bind everything together.

TO MAKE THE BREAKFAST BARS

1. Preheat your oven to 350°F.
2. Add the banana, peanut butter, almond milk, and maple syrup to a large bowl and stir to combine.
3. Now add in the oats, ground almonds, seeds, cinnamon, and parchment paper.
4. Stir everything really well to combine.
5. Now fold in the berries. Don't mix too much!
6. Line your baking tray with baking paper, then add the mix to the bottom. Press into the corners, top with more fruit and nuts—press in a little.
7. Bake for about 20 minutes.
8. Allow to cool a little before eating—if you can!

INGREDIENTS

Strawberry smoothie bowl

½ cup strawberries, fresh or frozen

2 ripe frozen bananas

Handful of spinach

1 tbsp nut butter

2 tbsp plant-based yogurt

Oat & berry smoothie

½ ripe banana

3 tbsp oats

½ cup plant-based milk

1 tbsp nut butter

⅓ cup blueberries—or any berry, fresh or frozen

Tropical smoothie

½ cup mango or pineapple—fresh or frozen

½ ripe banana

½ cup plant-based milk

Handful of spinach

1 tbsp nut butter of your choice

1 tbsp plant-based yogurt

Three delicious fruit smoothies

Smoothies are a great way to add fresh fruit to your day (and maybe a few greens too). Both the tropical and berry smoothies can be made in a standard blender, but you'll need a high-speed blender or food processor for the smoothie bowl to make it super creamy.

TO MAKE THE SMOOTHIE BOWL

1. Peel and chop your bananas and pop them in a freezer bag and freeze overnight.
2. Add the bananas and all the other ingredients to your food processor or high-speed blender and blend until really smooth and creamy. You may need to scrape the mixture off the sides a few times.

TO MAKE THE SMOOTHIES

Add everything to your blender and blend until smooth and creamy.

Niki's tip
You can top all of these delicious smoothies with fruit, seeds, or granola for more crunch.

Toast toppers

Smashed peas with toasted seeds

For the smashed peas:

1 ½ cups frozen peas

Big handful fresh mint leaves

Juice ½ lemon

½ tsp salt

1 ½ tbsp extra virgin olive oil

Twist of black pepper

2 tbsp seeds— sunflower or pumpkin

Crushed butter beans with tomato & basil

1 can butter beans drained

2 tbsp extra virgin olive oil

Pinch of sea salt

Juice ¼ lemon

Handful cherry tomatoes sliced in half or 2 tomatoes sliced

Handful fresh basil

Peanut butter & fruit

2 tbsp peanut butter or any nut butter

Handful berries of choice

2 slices of toast

I love toast! It's one of the quickest meals, but that doesn't mean it can't be exciting. Here are three tasty ideas, but the options are endless and you can mix and match toppings. All of these delicious toasts are great for breakfast or lunch.

TO MAKE THE SMASHED PEAS

1. Firstly defrost the peas by adding them to a sieve and running them under warm water.
2. Add the peas to a food processor and blend to a chunky mash, or place the peas into a tub and crush roughly with a fork.
3. Add in the rest of the ingredients and stir. Blend or crush again briefly to mix everything in.
4. To dry toast the seeds, add them to a pan and heat on a medium heat until lightly toasted. Be careful not to burn them, as they can blacken easily!

TO MAKE THE CRUSHED BUTTER BEANS

1. Add all the ingredients to a bowl and mix, then crush roughly.
2. Top with tomato and basil.

Niki's tip

Add toasted nuts and seeds, slices of avocado, or crispy tofu for extra plant-based protein.

Makes 8-10 bowls

Wet ingredients

4 tbsp maple syrup

4 tbsp chunky peanut
butter or nut butter

Dry ingredients

5 tbsp desiccated
coconut

1 cup oats

3 tbsp ground almonds

2 tbsp flour

1 tsp cinnamon

5 tbsp seeds—
your choice

4 tbsp sliced almonds

1 cup pecans

Pecan pie granola

In the mood for some weekend baking? You could make a big batch of my pecan pie granola on the weekend so you can have a ready-made and tasty breakfast during the week. It's perfect with some plant-based milk—but even better with added fruit and yogurt. It's a delicious topping for vegan ice cream as well!

TO MAKE THE GRANOLA

1. Preheat your oven to 325°F.

2. Mix the dry ingredients together in a bowl.

3. Now add in the maple syrup and peanut butter.

4. Mix thoroughly with your hands until the mixture is crumbly.

5. Spread the mix out on a large baking tray.

6. Bake for 25-30 minutes or until lightly toasted—give it a stir halfway through. Keep an eye on it to make sure it doesn't burn.

7. Set aside to cool down.

8. Transfer to airtight jars to store.

Niki's tip

This is great as a portable snack—portion into small bags to take with you.

For the pancakes

¾ cup plain flour

½ tsp cinnamon

1 tsp baking powder

1 small ripe banana

¾ cup plant-based milk of your choice

1-2 tsp maple syrup

Oil for frying if needed

For the caramelized bananas

2 ripe bananas

2 tbsp vegetable oil or coconut oil

Other topping ideas

Plant-based yogurt

Peanut butter

Berry compôte

Chopped nuts

Sweet morning banana pancakes

You don't need eggs to make deliciously fluffy pancakes—these ones are all about the bananas. There are bananas inside to give sweetness, and it's topped with amazing gooey caramelized bananas too—delicious!

TO MAKE THE PANCAKES

1. Add the flour, cinnamon, baking powder, almond milk, banana, and maple syrup to a bowl and mix thoroughly to form a thick batter.

2. Spoon a dessert spoon of the mixture into a nonstick pan. Add as many more as you can fit in the pan without them touching. Fry for 1-2 minutes until little bubbles form on the top.

3. Carefully flip the pancakes and then cook for another minute or so, until the pancakes are cooked through and slightly golden.

4. Repeat with all the mixture and set aside on a plate.

TO MAKE THE CARAMELIZED BANANAS

1. Chop the top end off the bananas. Carefully slice through the middle, lengthwise. Peel the bananas.

2. Add the oil to a pan and bring it to a medium heat.

3. Add the banana slices and fry in the oil on one side until they're browned, then flip over to caramelize the other side.

4. Add to the pancakes and serve.

Niki's tip

Simmer some raspberries with a tbsp of maple syrup to make a topping.

Niki's tip

Why not try toasties with hummus and roast veggies, mushroom and cheese, or peanut butter and banana?

INGREDIENTS
Makes 2 toasties

For the pesto, cheese, and avocado toastie

4 slices bread

Drizzle of olive oil or vegan butter

Filling

2 tbsp vegan pesto— see page 61

½ avocado

4 tbsp grated vegan cheese or 3 tbsp nut cheese

For the tomato pizza toastie

4 slices bread

Drizzle of olive oil or vegan butter

Filling

2 tbsp tomato purée

4 cherry tomatoes, sliced

4 tbsp grated vegan cheese or 3 tbsp nut cheese

Ultimate "cheese" toasties

I love a cheese toastie! Gooey melting cheese and crispy toast are seriously delicious. Thankfully vegans don't have to miss out! Use either store-bought vegan cheese or homemade nut cheese. Choose from pesto, cheese, and avocado toasties, or tomato pizza flavor toasties.

TO MAKE THE TOASTIES

1. Heat a griddle or frying pan to a medium heat.
2. Drizzle some olive oil or spread some vegan spread over one side of two slices of bread. Place them oil/spread side onto the pan and then top with the pesto/tomato paste.
3. Next add the grated vegan cheese and the avocado/ sliced cherry tomatoes.
4. Allow to cook for 2-3 minutes until the base has browned a little.
5. Now place the other two slices on top and press down a bit.
6. Drizzle with more olive oil or spread with butter. Carefully flip over so the uncooked side is now on the pan.
7. Cook for a further 2-3 minutes until that side has browned.
8. Remove from the pan and slice.

LUNCH

Liven up your lunchbox with these vibrant vegan recipes—they're so easy to make.

Pea & avocado dip

1 cup frozen peas

Handful of fresh mint

½ avocado

Juice ½ lemon

2 tbsp olive oil

½ tsp salt

2 tbsp tahini—optional

Creamy bean hummus dip

1 can butter beans or chickpeas, drained

Juice ½ lemon

1 clove garlic

2 tbsp olive oil

½ tsp sea salt

2 tbsp tahini

Red pepper dip

1 jar roasted red peppers in oil or brine, drained and rinsed

¾ cup walnuts

1 tsp cumin seeds

1 tsp smoked paprika

Juice ½ lemon

1 tsp sea salt

Twist of black pepper

1 tbsp olive oil

Quick dips

All these dips are scrumptious on toast, sandwiches, or jacket potatoes. My lovely sweet pea and avocado dip is one of my favourites and can be whipped up in a few minutes—you can dollop it on toast for a speedy lunch. The red pepper dip is also great as a quick pasta sauce!

TO MAKE THE PEA DIP

1. Defrost the peas by putting them in a sieve and running them under a warm tap.
2. Add all the ingredients to a food processor or blender and blitz briefly to a chunky mash.

TO MAKE THE CREAMY BEAN HUMMUS DIP

1. Add the butter beans to your blender or food processor with the garlic, lemon juice, tahini, and olive oil.
2. Blend until smooth and creamy (about 2 minutes), add a little water to loosen.
3. Season to taste and blend again.

TO MAKE THE RED PEPPER DIP

1. Dry toast the walnuts in a pan until lightly toasted. Set aside.
2. Add the walnuts to a food processor and blend to a chunky crumb.
3. Add the rest of the ingredients to your food processor and blend to a chunky paste.

Easy roast vegetables, chickpea, & rice salad with tahini dressing

This tasty salad is easy to make—just roast some veggies, mix with cooked rice and chickpeas, and stir in the dressing. Perfect for a packed lunch!

TO MAKE THE SALAD

1. Cook the rice according to the packet instructions. Allow to cool.

2. Preheat your oven to 350°F.

3. Chop up the zucchini and pepper and then add to a baking tray with the oil and a little salt. Roast for 25-30 minutes until cooked. Allow to cool.

4. To toast the seeds—add the seeds to a frying pan and dry fry for a few minutes on a medium heat until lightly toasted (be careful not to burn them). Set aside.

5. Add all the dressing ingredients to a jar and mix.

6. In a large bowl, mix the rice, chickpeas, roast vegetables, tomatoes, and seeds. Season well and dress with the dressing.

7. Divide into lunch boxes and keep in the fridge.

INGREDIENTS

For the salad
1 cup pasta, cooked
Handful of cherry tomatoes, sliced

For the pesto
2 cups fresh basil leaves
¾ cup pine nuts
1 clove of garlic
Juice ½ lemon
3 tbsp olive oil
3 tbsp nutritional yeast
¼ cup water

For the walnut bacon
2 tsp smoked paprika
1 tsp ground cumin
1 tsp balsamic vinegar
1 tsp maple syrup
1 big pinch of salt
¾ cup walnuts

Pesto pasta salad

Make a big batch of this pesto pasta on the weekend and then you can use pantry ingredients like butter beans, sundried tomatoes, or olives to jazz it up.

TO MAKE THE PESTO
Add all the ingredients to a food processor and blend to a paste. Transfer to a jar.

TO MAKE THE WALNUT "BACON"
1. Toast the walnuts in a pan over a medium heat for 5-6 minutes until they are lightly toasted – be careful not to burn them!
2. Add the cooked walnuts and spices to a food processor along with the balsamic vinegar, maple syrup, and a pinch of salt.
3. Blend for a minute or two until the walnut mixture turns into a crumbly texture.

TO SERVE
1. Toss the pesto with cooked pasta. Store in a large container in the fridge.
2. When adding to your lunch box, top with the walnut "bacon" and cherry tomatoes.

INGREDIENTS

Cooked pasta
½ cup per portion

Roast peppers
1 red pepper
1 yellow pepper
1 tbsp olive oil
Pinch salt

For the spinach pesto
⅓ cup hazelnuts or walnuts
3 tbsp toasted pine nuts
3 handfuls of spinach
1 handful of basil
Juice ½ lemon
½ tsp sea salt
1 clove of garlic
3 tbsp nutritional yeast
2 tbsp olive oil
3 oz water

This recipe is designed to give you some ideas to create your own quick bowls for easy packed lunches. This recipe is for roast peppers and spinach pesto, but you can make your own combination using the table below for inspiration.

TO ROAST THE PEPPERS

1. Preheat your oven to 350°F.
2. Slice the peppers then add to a large baking tray.
3. Toss with olive oil and salt.
4. Bake for around 30 minutes, then remove from the oven.
5. Cook the pasta as per pack instructions. Drain and set aside.

TO MAKE THE SPINACH PESTO

Add all the ingredients to a food processor and blend to a paste, then transfer to a jar.

MIX & MATCH PASTA IDEAS

FRESH
1 portion
Roast veggies
4 cherry tomatoes

+

PROTEIN
1 portion
2 cooked veggie sausages
3 tbsp mixed beans
3 tbsp corn
Cooked smoked tofu
3 tbsp cooked peas

+

SAUCE
1 portion
2 tbsp pesto
—see page 61
2 tbsp tomato sauce—see page 72

+

CRUNCH
1 portion
Seeds—1 tbsp—sunflower, pumpkin
Nuts—1 tbsp—walnuts, hazelnuts

Niki's tip
If you have any leftover roast veggies, add them to a salad or savory dish.

INGREDIENTS
Makes 2 wraps

....

The wraps

2 wraps of choice

1 onion

2 peppers

1 zucchini

1 eggplant

Tzatziki

½ cucumber, grated

120g plant-based or coconut yogurt

2 tbsp chopped dill

1 tbsp chopped fresh mint

Juice ¼ lemon

1 clove garlic, minced

½ tsp sea salt

Twist of black pepper

1 tbsp olive oil—optional

Dip

6 tbsp hummus/pea dip/ red pepper dip

Fresh veggies

1 grated carrot

4 cherry tomatoes

Crunch

1 tbsp toasted sunflower/pumpkin seeds

Loaded roast veggie wraps with hummus and tzatziki

Perfect for a packed lunch, these versatile wraps can be stuffed with any of your favorite fillings. I've gone for roast veggies and hummus, topped with the most amazing homemade tzatziki.

TO MAKE THE ROAST VEGGIES

1. Preheat your oven to 350°F.
2. Chop up the veggies into big pieces, and add to a large baking tray.
3. Drizzle over the oil and sprinkle with the salt.
4. Bake for around 25-30 minutes, or until soft and cooked through. Set aside.

TO MAKE THE TZATZIKI

1. Grate the cucumber and pop it into a large sieve to drain over a bowl. Squeeze out as much moisture as possible, then transfer to a large bowl.
2. Add all the other ingredients and mix well.
3. Add a drizzle of olive oil on top to finish it off.

TO SERVE

1. Load the wraps with hummus or your choice of dip.
2. Add the roast veg, grated carrots, and cherry tomatoes.
3. Dollop on some tzatziki and seeds.
4. Wrap everything tightly.

2 tbsp olive oil

1 onion

2 cloves of garlic

1 tsp ground cumin

1 tsp turmeric

1 tsp ground coriander

3 small sweet potatoes, peeled and chopped into small cubes

2 cups vegetable stock

1 can coconut milk

1 tbsp tomato purée

Twist of black pepper

½ tsp salt

Toppings

Toasted seeds or nuts

A swirl of plant-based yogurt

Pinch of chili flakes (if you like some spice!)

Creamy sweet potato soup

This soup is creamy, smooth, and lovely. It's lightly flavored with some Indian spices, and really easy to make.

TO MAKE THE SOUP

1. Finely dice the onion, and chop the garlic up as well.
2. Add the onion to a large pan with the olive oil and sauté for 7-8 minutes on a low heat. Add in the spices and garlic and fry for a further few minutes.
3. Next add the sweet potato, stock, coconut milk, and tomato purée to the pan and simmer for 15 minutes covered—until the sweet potato is soft. Season with salt and pepper.
4. Turn off the heat and then blend using a hand blender, until smooth and creamy.
5. Add more water if you'd like it thinner.

TO SERVE

Top with the toasted seeds and plant-based yogurt.

1 tbsp olive oil

1 onion

2 cloves of garlic

1 tbsp smoked paprika

4 large ripe tomatoes, chopped

2 tbsp tomato purée

2 cups vegetable stock

1 can cannellini beans, drained

1 can butter beans, drained

1 tsp salt

1 tsp white wine/cider vinegar

2 handfuls of spinach

Toppings
Pine nuts or toasted seeds

Speedy smoky tomato & bean soup

This tasty and easy soup is perfect for splitting into batches for lunch boxes or freezing for when you need it. And you can literally use any beans you have in the cupboard—pick your favorite! The paprika adds lots of smoky flavor.

TO MAKE THE SOUP

1. Roughly chop the onion, and finely chop or grate the garlic.
2. In a large pan, cook the onion in the oil on a medium heat for about 7-8 minutes until soft.
3. Add the garlic and paprika to the mix, and cook for a further minute.
4. Now add in the chopped tomatoes and tomato purée, then cook for a few minutes until they are soft.
5. Add the stock. Simmer for 10 minutes.
6. Add in the beans, spinach, vinegar, salt, and pepper. Cook for a further few minutes until the spinach has wilted.

MAIN MEALS

Whether you're making a meal for one
or preparing food for your whole family,
there's something for everyone here.

Niki's tip

Serve with plant-based yogurt, vegan cheese, and avocado for the ultimate nachos!

INGREDIENTS
Serves 4

. . . .

For the bean chili

1 onion, chopped

2 tbsp olive oil

3 cloves of garlic, grated

1 tbsp smoked paprika

1 tsp harissa paste

2 tbsp tomato purée

1 can chopped tomatoes

2 red peppers, chopped

1 can chickpeas/butter
beans, drained

1 can red kidney beans/
black beans, drained

1 small can of corn,
drained

1 tsp sea salt

Black pepper

1 tbsp chili flakes

Veggie ground beef –
optional

Nachos

2 tortilla wraps

1 tbsp olive oil
or use an oil spray

Bean chili nacho platter

A big pot of bean chili is always a crowd-pleaser—
packed with beans and delicious smoky flavor.
Have you made homemade nachos from tortilla
wraps before? It's really easy, and you can flavor
them with a little spice and top with cheese.

TO MAKE THE CHILI

1. Add the oil to a large saucepan, then add in the
   onion. Fry for 8-10 minutes on a medium heat until
   soft.
2. Add in the garlic and spices and cook for a further
   few minutes.
3. Add the harissa paste and tomato purée and stir.
4. Now add in the tomatoes and pepper, and simmer
   on a low heat for 10 minutes.
5. Add the beans and corn and stir, plus vegan ground
   beef if you like. Cook for another 5 minutes.
6. Season with salt and pepper.

TO MAKE THE NACHOS

1. Preheat your oven to 350°F.
2. Cut the wraps into triangles so you have 8 per
   wrap—a pizza cutter works well! Place on a
   baking tray.
3. Brush with oil and sprinkle with smoked paprika.
4. Bake for 10 minutes until crisp.

Flatbread base
5 oz white self-rising flour
1 tsp baking powder
2 tbsp plant-based yogurt
⅓ cup water

For the mushroom, tomato, & cheese pizza
3-4 mushrooms, sliced
1 tbsp olive oil
Vegan cheese of choice

For the pesto & cherry tomato pizza
Handful of cherry tomatoes, sliced

For the basil pesto
2 cups fresh basil leaves
¾ cup pine nuts
1 clove garlic, peeled
Juice ½ lemon
3 tbsp olive oil
3 tbsp nutritional yeast
¼ cup water

For the sundried tomato sauce
10 oz soft sundried tomatoes, drained
2 tbsp tomato purée
Pinch of salt
2 tsp cider vinegar
3 tbsp water

Mini flatbread pizzas with all the toppings

These mini flatbread pizzas are fun to make and you can add any of your favourite toppings. The fluffy flatbreads are so fast to make too.

TO MAKE THE FLATBREAD DOUGH

1. In a large bowl, add the flour and baking powder, and stir.
2. Add the water and yogurt, and mix thoroughly to combine. Knead for a minute until you get a springy dough. You might need to add a bit more water or flour so the dough isn't too wet or too dry.

TO MAKE THE PESTO OR TOMATO SAUCE

Add all the ingredients to a food processor and blend to a paste. Transfer to a jar.

TO MAKE THE MUSHROOMS

Slice the mushrooms then add them to a small pan with the olive oil. Fry for 4-5 minutes until soft. Set aside.

TO COOK THE FLATBREAD

1. Heat a large griddle or frying pan to medium.
2. Divide the dough into four then roll out the first flatbread onto a floured cutting board.
3. Pop it on to the griddle or frying pan and allow to cook and char a little on that side, then flip to cook on the other side. Repeat for each flatbread.

TO FINISH

Top the flatbreads with toppings above.

Niki's tip
For more toppings,
try pineapple chunks,
sundried tomatoes,
corn, roast veggies,
vegan pepperoni,
or olives.

Niki's tip

The tofu adds lots of plant-based protein, and pan-frying it makes it taste amazing.

INGREDIENTS
Serves 4

....

For the crispy tofu

14 oz natural firm tofu, cut into cubes

1 tbsp vegetable oil

For the peanut satay dressing

5 tbsp chunky peanut butter

Juice of 1 lime

1 tsp garlic powder

2 tbsp soy sauce

3 tbsp toasted sesame oil

1 tsp maple syrup

4 tbsp water

Pinch of chili flakes

For the stir-fry

1 tbsp veg oil

1 onion

3 cloves of garlic

1 red pepper

½ cup broccoli

½ cup sugar snap peas

½ zucchini

12 oz straight to wok vegan noodles

Toppings

Toasted peanuts or cashews

Stir-fried veggies & crispy tofu with peanut noodles

For years, a big veggie stir-fry was my go-to meal as it's so quick and easy to make. This recipe transforms it into something really special with this incredible peanut satay sauce.

TO MAKE THE TOFU

1. Drain and slice the tofu into large cubes.
2. Heat the oil in a large frying pan or wok.
3. Fry the tofu for a few minutes each side until brown and crispy, then transfer to a plate.

TO MAKE THE SATAY SAUCE

1. Add the ingredients to a jar and mix well to combine.

TO MAKE THE STIR-FRY

1. Roughly chop the onion and slice the garlic.
2. Heat a large frying pan to medium then add the oil.
3. Add the onion and fry for 7-8 minutes until soft and browning, then add the garlic.
4. Roughly chop all the veggies, then add to the pan.
5. Fry for 3-4 minutes until the veggies are cooked but still crunchy.
6. Add the noodles and peanut sauce, stir to combine, and cook for a further minute.
7. Now add the crispy tofu and stir it in carefully.
8. Serve topped with toasted nuts.

Serves 4

• •

For the crispy chickpeas

1 can chickpeas, drained

1 tsp vegetable/olive oil

1 tsp garam masala or ground coriander

½ tsp turmeric

Pinch of salt

For the curry

1 onion

1 tbsp olive oil

3 cloves of garlic

1 tsp ground turmeric

1 tsp cumin seeds

1 tsp ground coriander

5 tomatoes chopped roughly, plus ¾ cup water—or 1 can tomatoes

2 tbsp coconut cream or plant-based yogurt

14 oz frozen peas

½ tsp salt

Pinch of chili flakes—optional

To serve

1 ¼ cups cooked rice

Pea curry & crispy chickpea Indian bowl

I love this easy curry: it's a staple in my house. The great thing is, it's made from pantry ingredients so you can whip it up really easily. Peas and chickpeas are packed with lots of plant-based proteins, so it's not only delicious but healthy too!

TO MAKE THE CHICKPEAS

1. Preheat your oven to 350°F.
2. Add all the ingredients to a bowl and mix to combine. Now transfer to a baking tray lined with parchment paper, and spread it all out.
3. Pop in the oven and roast for 15 minutes, or until crispy.

TO MAKE THE CURRY

1. First prep your veggies: chop the onion up roughly and slice the garlic.
2. Add the onion and oil to a large saucepan and fry for about 8-10 minutes until soft and browning a little.
3. While the onions are browning, start cooking your rice according to the packet instructions.
4. Add the spices and the garlic to the onions and stir for another couple of minutes, then add in the chopped tomatoes.
5. Turn up the heat to medium, add the water and cook for a further 10 minutes.
6. Now add the peas, coconut yogurt, salt, and chili flakes, and stir to combine. Allow to warm through, then serve with the crispy chickpeas and the rice.

Niki's tip

If you don't have all the dried spices you can use curry paste—use one tablespoon instead.

Niki's tip

If you don't want to use tofu, you could just add in more veggies. Eggplant, zucchini and more peppers are perfect.

Loaded tofu fajitas

I love this recipe—it has crispy tofu and lots of delicious spiced veggies, all wrapped up in warm tortillas. Delicious! The key to crispy tofu? Cooking the tofu in a pan separately makes it crispy on the outside and gooey on the inside. So good.

TO COOK THE TOFU

1. Slice the tofu into large cubes.
2. In a separate large frying pan, heat 1 teaspoon of oil to a medium heat, then add the tofu to the pan.
3. Fry the tofu for a few minutes each side until brown and crispy, then transfer to a plate. Make sure all sides are lightly brown.

TO MAKE THE FAJITAS

1. Heat oven to 350°F and wrap 4 medium tortillas in foil.
2. Slice the onion into strips then add it along with the oil to a frying pan. Fry on a medium heat for 7-8 minutes until soft.
3. Now add the spices to the onions and stir to combine.
4. Chop up the pepper and cherry tomatoes and add them to the pan. Cook for 4-5 minutes until the tomatoes have softened.
5. Add the corn and tofu and season with the salt and carefully stir to combine.
6. Put the tortillas in the oven to heat up and serve with the tofu mix.
7. Top with sliced avocado, plant-based yogurt, fresh coriander, and a squeeze of lime.

....

1 red onion

2 tbsp olive oil

2 cloves of garlic, grated

1 tbsp smoked paprika

2 cans chopped tomatoes

1 small jar sundried tomatoes

1 tsp soy sauce

1 tsp maple syrup

1 can cannelloni beans, drained—or chickpeas, butter beans, kidney, or black beans

1 tsp sea salt

Pinch of black pepper

12 vegan sausages of your choice

Veggie sausage & bean bake

This is a crowd-pleaser of a meal—great for lunch, dinner, or even breakfast. The beans and tomatoes make a tasty sauce with your favorite store-bought vegan sausages. Serve with crispy potatoes or fresh bread to mop up the sauce.

1. Chop up the onion and crush the garlic.

2. Add your oil and onion to a wide bottom pan and fry gently on a low heat for around 10 minutes until soft and browning.

3. Add the garlic and fry for 30 seconds more.

4. Add the smoked paprika. Stir to combine.

5. Now drain the sundried tomatoes into a bowl and chop them up. Add them to the pan along with the canned tomatoes and cook on a low heat for 5 minutes.

6. Preheat your oven to 350°F.

7. Add the soy sauce, maple syrup, salt, black pepper, and beans to the pan. Turn off the heat.

8. Add the vegan sausages along with a splash of oil to a large frying pan and fry for a few minutes on each side until a little colored.

9. You can now add the sausages along with the tomato mix to a large casserole dish.

10. Transfer to your oven and bake for 15 minutes.

Niki's tip

Make the dish even tastier by adding some vegan cheese to the top before baking.

Niki's tip

I used chickpeas for the meatless balls, but black beans are also great.

INGREDIENTS
Makes 18-20 balls

For the meatless balls

1 onion

2 oz walnuts

1 can chickpeas, drained

⅓ cup rolled oats

1 tsp garlic powder

½ cup cooked brown or white rice

2 tbsp tomato ketchup

1 tbsp smoked paprika

1 tbsp soy sauce

1 tsp salt

For the tomato sauce

1 red onion

2 tbsp olive oil

3 garlic cloves, crushed

1 tsp smoked paprika or sweet paprika

1 can tomatoes, blended

1 tbsp tomato purée

1 tsp sea salt

Pinch of chili flakes—optional

Twist of black pepper

To serve

½ cup tagliatelle per person

Fresh basil

Vegan cheese

Meatless balls tagliatelle

My meatless balls are fun to make and a great family meal. Chunky balls, a rich tomato sauce, and tasty pasta—what's not to like?

TO MAKE THE BALLS

1. Chop the onion finely. Now add the onion to a small saucepan with the olive oil and fry on a medium heat until soft and slightly browned—for about 8 minutes.
2. Add the walnuts to a small pan and fry on a medium heat until lightly toasted. Be careful not to burn them!
3. Now add the onions, walnuts and all the remaining ingredients to a food processor and blend to a chunky paste.
4. Heat a large frying pan to medium and add a little oil. Use your hands to scoop out and form the meatball mixture into inch-wide balls. Fry them until golden brown on all sides—about 10 minutes in total.

TO MAKE THE TOMATO SAUCE

1. Add your oil and onion to a wide bottom pan and fry gently on a low heat for around 10 minutes until soft and browning. Add the garlic and fry for 30 seconds more.
2. Add the smoked paprika. Stir to combine.
3. Now add the blended canned tomatoes and tomato purée to the pan and cook on a low heat for 10 minutes.
4. Add the salt, black pepper, and optional chili flakes, and simmer for a further minute.

TO SERVE

1. Cook the tagliatelle according to pack instructions.
2. Toss the tagliatelle in the tomato sauce. Top with the meatless balls, plus basil and vegan cheese if you like.

For the falafel burgers

1 can chickpeas, rinsed and drained

1 small red onion

1 tsp garlic powder

1 tsp smoked paprika

1 tsp ground cumin

½ - 1 tsp harissa paste

Pinch of salt

Twist of pepper

2 tbsp plain flour

2 tbsp vegetable oil

4 buns of choice

Toppings

4 tbsp vegan mayonnaise

Handful of salad leaves

3 slices pickle per burger

4 tbsp hummus— store-bought or according to the recipe on page 59

2 tomatoes, sliced

Harissa falafel burger

My falafel burgers are easy to make and so tasty! The burgers tick all the boxes—crispy and lightly spiced falafels, layered with creamy mayonnaise, crispy salad, hummus, tomatoes, and pickles (optional—but I love them!). They're great in a burger bun, but also delicious in a pita or served with crispy potatoes.

TO MAKE THE BURGERS

1. Chop up the onion roughly then add along with all the remaining ingredients to a food processor. Blitz to a chunky paste.

2. Heat a large frying pan to medium and add a little oil. Scoop out and form the burger mixture into a ball, then flatten to a burger patty shape in your hand.

3. Pop in the pan and fry until golden brown on both sides—about 4-5 minutes on each side.

TO SERVE

Layer the mayonnaise then salad onto the base of the bun, top with the falafel burger then add sliced tomatoes and pickles. Spread hummus inside the top half of the bun. Squeeze the two halves together and take a bite!

Niki's tip

Other delicious burger toppings include vegan cheese, tzatziki, chilis, and onion rings.

Serves 4

....

For the curry

1 tbsp olive oil

1 onion

1 tsp ground turmeric

1 tsp cumin seeds or ground cumin

1 tsp ground coriander

½ tsp chili flakes—optional

2 cloves of garlic

Thumb-size piece of ginger

4 ripe tomatoes

1 large sweet potato, peeled

1 can coconut milk

1 can cooked chickpeas, drained

1 tsp salt

Twist of black pepper

Handful of spinach and/or coriander

Toppings

Coriander

3 tbsp cashews/peanuts

To serve

1 ½ cups cooked rice

Quick creamy chickpea & sweet potato curry

This creamy curry made with sweet potato, chickpeas, and coconut milk is so good. You'll love it with fluffy rice or flatbreads. Why not serve it with more curry dishes for a big curry feast?

TO MAKE THE CURRY

1. Chop up the onion roughly and grate the garlic and the ginger.
2. Now add the oil to a large pan and heat to a medium heat. Add the onion and fry for about 7-8 minutes until soft and browning.
3. Now add the garlic, ginger, and spices and stir for another couple of minutes.
4. In the meantime, chop up the tomatoes and chop the sweet potato into small cubes, then add to the pan and cook for a further 2-3 minutes, stirring occasionally until the tomatoes have softened.
5. Now add the chickpeas and coconut milk. Simmer for 15-20 minutes, until the sweet potato is tender.
6. Throw in some spinach, coriander, salt, and pepper and stir so the greens wilt in.

TO TOAST YOUR CASHEWS OR PEANUTS

In a dry pan, add the cashews and heat on a medium heat until lightly toasted. Be careful not to burn them!

TO SERVE

Serve with rice, and top with toasted nuts and coriander.

For the "cheesy" potato topping

1 large sweet potato

1 large white potato

Pinch of salt

2 tbsp coconut yogurt or other plant-based yogurt

3 tbsp nutritional yeast

1 tsp salt

Twist of black pepper

For the filling

1 leek

1 tbsp olive oil

2 cloves of garlic, sliced

1 tbsp smoked paprika

2 tbsp tomato purée

⅔ cup red lentils, rinsed

3 cups vegetable stock – vegan bouillon is best

1 tbsp balsamic vinegar

1 can black beans, drained

Twist of black pepper

Black bean & lentil bake with "cheesy" sweet potato mash

This one is perfect for cooking for your family. It's big and hearty and delicious—perfect for a Sunday lunch with roast vegetables and gravy. The delicious fluffy mash topping can be made with all sweet potato or white potato—your choice. But sweet potato has more nutrients.

TO MAKE THE TOPPING

1. Peel and chop the potatoes into small cubes. Add them to a pan of boiling water with a pinch of salt.
2. Cook on a high simmer for about 10 minutes until soft. Allow to cool a little, then drain the potatoes.
3. Add them to a large bowl, then mash roughly. Add the other topping ingredients, mix well, and set aside.

TO MAKE THE FILLING

1. Roughly chop the leek, add to a large pan with the oil and fry on a medium heat for 5-6 minutes until soft.
2. Add in the garlic and stir for another few minutes. Add the smoked paprika and tomato purée.
3. Now add the lentils, vegetable stock, and balsamic vinegar.
4. Bring to the boil then down the heat to low and simmer for 15 minutes. Add a bit more water if needed.
5. Now add the black beans and black pepper and stir.

TO PUT THE DISH TOGETHER

1. Preheat your oven to 350°F.
2. Add the lentils mix to a medium casserole dish, spread out over the base.
3. Top with the mash, spreading out to cover everything. Score the top with a fork.
4. Bake for 20 minutes, until the top is crispy.

Niki's tip

No black beans? Use red kidney beans or any small bean. You can also portion it up and freeze for future meals.

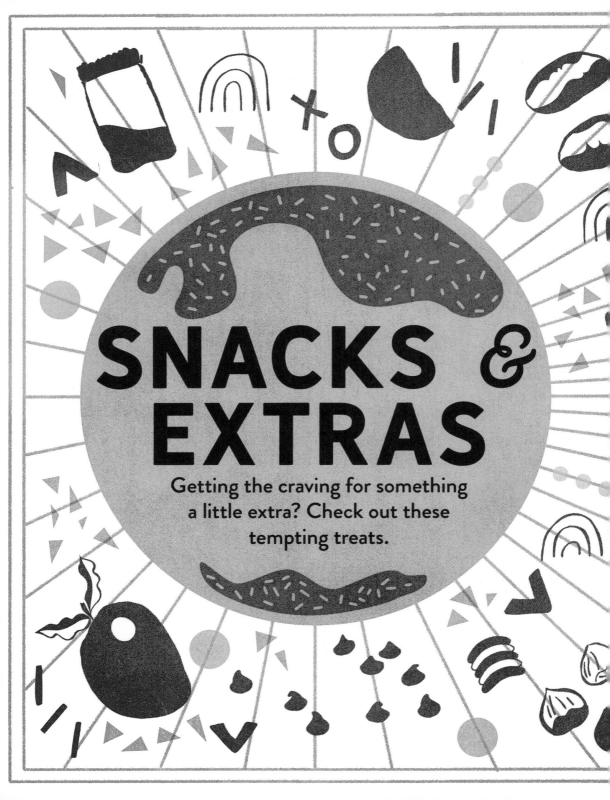

SNACKS & EXTRAS

Getting the craving for something a little extra? Check out these tempting treats.

For the red pepper dip

6 oz jar roast peppers in oil or brine, drained

1 tsp smoked paprika or sweet paprika

Pinch of salt

1 tsp maple syrup

½ tsp harissa paste

For the corn fritters

1 ¼ cups plain flour

1 tsp baking powder

1 tsp garlic powder

Pinch of salt

Pinch of black pepper

1 tbsp nutritional yeast—optional

1 cup water

1 red pepper, diced

2 spring onions, sliced

10 oz canned corn, drained

Oil for frying

Corn fritters with smoky red pepper dip

These sweet and tasty corn fritters are a winner. Dunking them in the smoky pepper dip is delicious, but dipping into multiple dips is better—try hummus, vegan mayonnaise or salsa.

TO MAKE THE SMOKY RED PEPPER DIP

1. Drain and rinse the roast peppers.
2. Add all the ingredients to a food processor or blender. Blend to a chunky paste.

TO MAKE THE FRITTERS

1. Add the flour, salt, pepper, garlic powder, and nutritional yeast to a large bowl. Stir to combine.
2. Add in the water and mix to a smooth batter. Add in the veggies and corn and stir well. Set aside for 10 minutes.
3. Add a little oil to the base of a non-stick small frying pan. Add a heaped tablespoon of the batter to the pan and flatten a little so you get a roundish pancake.
4. Cook on a medium heat for approximately 2 minutes until you can lift over to flip easily.
5. Flip and cook on the other side for around 1-2 minutes until cooked through.
6. Remove from the pan and place on a plate. Cover with a clean cloth to keep warm.
7. Repeat the process with the rest of the batter.

TO SERVE

Load the fritters with the pepper dip and dig in!

....

**For the
jackfruit filling**

1 red onion

2 tbsp olive oil

2 cloves of garlic

4 mushrooms

14 oz can jackfruit,
drained

1 tbsp soy sauce

5 tbsp hoisin sauce

1 tbsp toasted sesame oil

Black pepper

Pinch of chili flakes

For the wraps

4 wraps of your choice

1 ½ cups cooked rice

¼ cucumber, cut into
thin strips

2 tbsp vegan
mayonnaise

2 tbsp sesame seeds

Hoisin jackfruit burritos

You've got to try these! Delicious hoisin jackfruit,
rice, and vegan mayo all sandwiched together in
a tasty wrap. The jackfruit filling is great—but
another delicious option is cubes of roasted sweet
potato or squash.

TO MAKE THE FILLING

1. Chop the onion up roughly and slice the garlic. Slice
the mushrooms finely and chop the drained jackfruit
up a bit.

2. Add the oil to a medium pan. Add the onions and
fry for 6-8 minutes until soft and browning.

3. Add in the garlic and mushrooms, and cook for a
further 3 minutes.

4. Transfer the jackfruit, soy sauce, and hoisin to the
pan and stir to combine.

5. Cook for a further 5 minutes.

6. Finally add the toasted sesame oil, black pepper, and
chili flakes. Set aside.

TO SERVE

1. Lay out the wraps and then add the rice to
the middle, now layer the jackfruit, cucumber,
mayonnaise, and sesame seeds.

2. Fold the left and right sides in toward the filling,
then fold the top and bottom sides around the filling
to form your burrito.

Niki's tip

Want to know the best way to fold a burrito? There are lots of burrito folding videos on YouTube ... weird but true!

Niki's tip

Try swapping the hummus and smashed avocado for smashed peas or red pepper dip.

For the toasts

1 large eggplant
1 large sweet potato
Olive oil for rubbing
Pinch of salt

For the chickpeas

1 can chickpeas, drained
1 tbsp rose harissa or
1 tsp harissa paste
1 tbsp olive oil
Juice ½ lemon
1 tsp smoked paprika
Big pinch of salt

For smashed avocado

1 ripe avocado
Salt and pepper
Juice ¼ lemon

For the hummus

See page 59

Toppings

3 tbsp pomegranate seeds
Handful of arugula leaves

Sweet potato & eggplant toasts with smashed avocado & harissa chickpeas

A great snack to make for your friends. The sliced sweet potato and eggplant act as tasty and healthy toast alternatives—top with your favorite toppings and layer them up. I love smashed avocado, creamy hummus, and smoky chickpeas—delicious!

TO COOK THE EGGPLANT & SWEET POTATO

1. Preheat oven to 350°F.
2. Slice the aubergine lengthways (into about 4 slices) and the sweet potato lengthways (into about 6 slices), then rub in a little oil.
3. Add the eggplant and sweet potato to a lined baking tray, and sprinkle with salt.
4. Bake for 15 minutes then flip over and bake for 15 minutes more. Make sure they are tender, then remove from the oven and place on a serving plate.

TO MAKE THE CHICKPEAS

Add all the ingredients to a bowl and stir to combine.

TO MAKE THE AVOCADO

Mash your avocado in a bowl with salt, pepper, and lemon juice to taste.

TO SERVE

Top the eggplant and sweet potato with the avocado, hummus, harissa chickpeas, pomegranate, and leaves.

Niki's tip
Don't rush the rice wrapper soaking. Make sure they are soft before removing from the water.

INGREDIENTS

Makes 20 rolls

....

For the rolls

10 rice paper wrappers

1 red pepper

1 carrot

½ cucumber

1 ripe avocado

½ mango

½ cup cooked rice

1 tsp sriracha—optional

Handful of mint

Handful of coriander

For the peanut dip

1 tbsp soy sauce

1 tbsp toasted sesame oil

6 tbsp coconut milk

1 tsp maple syrup

3 tbsp chunky peanut butter

1 tsp garlic granules

½ tsp sriracha or chili flakes

For the sesame dressing

Juice ½ lime

1 tsp vegan brown sugar

1 tbsp tamari/soy

1 tbsp toasted sesame oil

Super summer rolls

Fresh, healthy, and fun to make, these vibrant summer rolls are a perfect snack. Once you've mastered soaking the wrappers and rolling, you'll want to make them all the time.

TO MAKE THE SUMMER ROLLS

1. Chop the pepper, cucumber, and carrots into strips. Slice, peel, and de-stone the avocado and mango and cut into slices.

2. Stir the sriracha into the cooked rice and get your mint and coriander ready.

3. Boil 2 cups of water and carefully pour into a flat dish.

4. Add one rice wrapper at a time to the water, submerge for about 20 seconds or until soft, then transfer to a clean plate.

5. Smooth out then add a strip of rice to the center along with a small amount of the other filling ingredients. Don't overfill.

6. Lift the edge of the wrapper nearest to you over the filling and, holding the filling in position with your fingers, start rolling up tightly.

7. When you're halfway, fold the ends of the rice paper in over the filling so that it is completely enclosed.

8. Keep on rolling tightly until the whole rice paper wrapper is rolled up. Repeat for the other wrappers.

TO MAKE THE PEANUT DIP

Add all the ingredients to a bowl and mix to combine.

TO MAKE THE SESAME DRESSING

Add all the ingredients to a bowl and mix to combine.

For the sweet potato filling

1 large sweet potato
Pinch of salt
1 tbsp olive oil
1 tsp smoked paprika
1 tsp harissa paste
Juice ½ lemon
½ tsp salt

To make the quesadilla

4 tortillas
8 mushrooms, sliced thinly
8 tbsp corn, drained
2 spring onions
2 oz vegan cheese

Sweet potato, mushroom, & corn quesadillas

These delicious quesadillas are great for sharing. The sweet potato mash is smoky and gooey, and mixed with corn, mushrooms, spring onions, and vegan cheese, it's a super tasty combination.

TO MAKE THE SWEET POTATO FILLING

1. Peel and chop the sweet potatoes into cubes.
2. Add to a pan with boiling salted water.
3. Simmer for 8-10 minutes or until tender. Remove from the heat and drain.
4. Add the sweet potato to a bowl along with the other ingredients. Using a fork, mash to combine well.

TO MAKE THE QUESADILLA

1. Lay the first tortilla onto the base of a large flat bottom pan or skillet. Cover the base with smashed sweet potato, then the mushrooms, spring onions, corn, and cheese.
2. Cover with the second tortilla and press down a little then turn onto a medium heat—allow the filling to heat through and the bottom tortilla to brown a little. This should take 3-4 minutes.
3. Carefully flip the quesadilla to brown the other side for 1 minute, then remove from the heat and onto a cutting board. Repeat with the next one.

Niki's tip

Try these fillings: hummus, roast peppers, vegan cheese and mushrooms, avocado and black beans.

Niki's tip
I love the taste of the protein-packed edamame, but you could use crushed toasted peanuts instead.

For the wedges

2 medium potatoes

1 small sweet potato, cleaned and cut into chunky wedges

1 tsp garlic powder

Pinch of sea salt

1 tbsp olive oil

For the garlic yogurt

3 tbsp plant-based yogurt

½ tsp garlic powder

Pinch of sea salt

1 tsp olive oil

1 tbsp lemon juice

Toppings

1 cup frozen edamame beans, defrosted by running them under hot water

2 tbsp sriracha, if you like it hot! Or ketchup/BBQ sauce

3 tbsp sesame seeds

Spicy wedges with all the toppings

Crispy potato and sweet potato wedges loaded with edamame, sriracha, creamy garlic yogurt & sesame seeds—ideal sharing food! Get your hands in and get a bit of everything with every mouthful.

TO MAKE THE WEDGES

1. Preheat your even to 350°F.
2. Cut the potatoes into long, chunky wedges.
3. Add them to a baking tray and sprinkle with garlic powder and sea salt. Drizzle with olive oil. Toss them to coat everything.
4. Bake for 50-60 minutes until crispy on the outside and soft inside.

TO MAKE THE GARLIC YOGURT

Add all the ingredients to a jar, and mix to combine.

TO SERVE

1. Add the wedges to a large plate, and cover with the edamame beans.
2. Dollop spoonfuls of the garlic yogurt on top.
3. Drizzle with sriracha, then sprinkle with sesame seeds to finish it off.

For the choc chip balls

2 oz ground almonds

1 cup dates—medjool is best

1 cup porridge oats

2 tbsp desiccated coconut

5 tbsp peanut butter

1 tsp cinnamon

1 tsp vanilla essence

Pinch of salt—optional

6 tbsp vegan choc chips

For the choc hazelnut truffles

½ cup hazelnuts or almonds

6-oz bar vegan chocolate

1 tbsp coconut oil

2 tbsp ground almonds

¾ cup pitted medjool dates

½ tsp vanilla essence

Pinch of sea salt

Peanut butter cookie choc chip balls & choc hazelnut truffles

These peanut butter cookie choc chip balls are like little cookies—ideal for an on-the-go snack. And these chocolate hazelnut truffles are a richly chocolatey treat. Both can be whipped up in minutes and last for a week or so.

TO MAKE THE CHOC CHIP BALLS

1. Add all the ingredients apart from the choc chips to a food processor. Blend until you get a sticky paste.
2. Now add the choc chips and blend again briefly to combine.
3. Scoop out bite-size pieces of the mix and roll into balls by squeezing together and rolling.

FOR THE TRUFFLES

1. Add the hazelnuts to your food processor and blend to a fine crumb.
2. Very gently melt the coconut oil and chocolate in a pan, then add to the processor.
3. Add all the remaining ingredients and blend until everything is combined.
4. Scoop out bite-size pieces of the truffle mix and roll into balls, pop in a container, and store in the fridge.

Niki's tip

Use medjool dates if you can get them as they're easier to blend— if not, soak dried dates for 30 minutes in warm water.

Niki's tip

Use any flour
you like for the
soda bread;
I like wholemeal
or spelt.

Quick flatbreads & soda bread

Impress your friends and family by making your own bread—both flatbreads and soda bread can be made quickly and easily, and fresh bread tastes and smells amazing!

TO MAKE THE FLATBREAD

1. In a large bowl, add the flour, baking powder, and salt and stir.
2. Now add the water and yogurt, mix thoroughly to combine, and then transfer to a floured board. You might need to add a bit more water or flour so the dough isn't too wet or too dry.
3. Knead for a few minutes until you get a springy dough.
4. Heat a large griddle or frying pan to a medium heat.
5. Divide the dough into four, then roll the first flatbread out on a floured cutting board.
6. Pop it on the pan and allow to cook and char a little on that side then flip it to cook on the other side. Repeat for each flatbread.

TO MAKE THE SODA BREAD

1. Preheat your oven to 400°F.
2. Mix all the dry ingredients together thoroughly in a large bowl. Add the almond milk, apple cider vinegar, and yogurt.
3. Stir until you get a smooth dough and then form into a ball. Place the ball on a floured baking tray and then cut a deep cross in the center. Sprinkle a few oats on the top.
4. Place the bread in your preheated oven for 35-40 minutes. Allow to cool for 10 minutes before slicing.

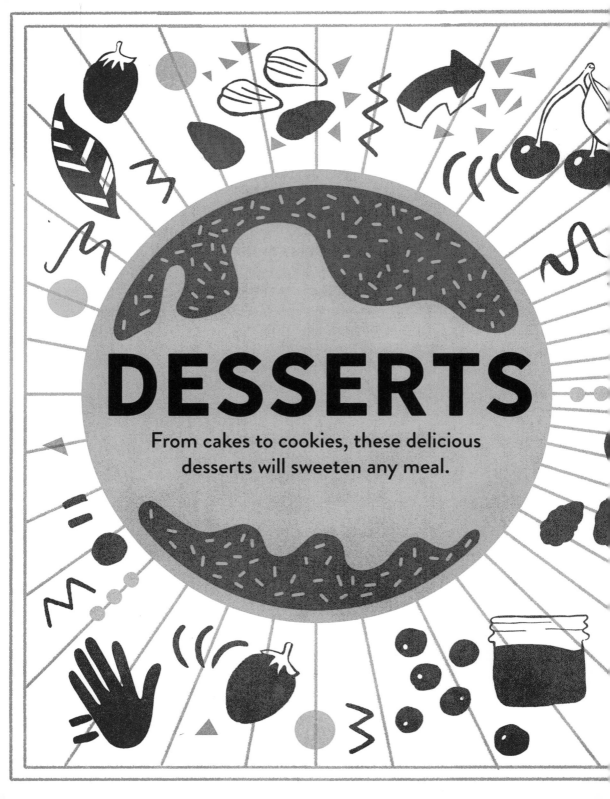

DESSERTS

From cakes to cookies, these delicious desserts will sweeten any meal.

For the base

6 oz ground almonds
6 medjool dates, pitted
3 tbsp coconut oil melted

For the caramel

20 medjool dates, pitted
3 tbsp almond butter
½ tsp vanilla essence
3 tbsp almond milk
Pinch sea salt

Chocolate layer

2 ½ oz vegan chocolate
3 tbsp coconut oil

Millionaire's shortbread slices

These delicious caramel slices just might be one of the best desserts I've made. It's a simple recipe but with maximum taste—a lovely biscuity base with a gooey caramel center and crispy chocolate on top. There's a real danger of wolfing them down, so chop them up and keep them in the freezer. And best of all, they can be eaten straight out of the freezer!

TO MAKE THE SLICES

1. Add all the base ingredients in your food processor and blend until everything comes together.

2. Line a small tray with parchment paper, then press the base mix firmly down and into the sides.

3. Wash the food processor, then add the caramel ingredients and blend until you get a super smooth paste. Spread this caramel mix over the base.

4. Break up the chocolate and place in a glass bowl with the coconut oil. Very gently melt over a saucepan of simmering water.

5. Pour the chocolate over the caramel, and then return to the fridge for at least 4 hours to firm up.

6. Slice as desired. Keep in the freezer if needed.

INGREDIENTS
Makes 6

. . . .

For the caramel

7 medjool dates, pitted

5 tbsp almond milk or plant-based milk of your choice

1 tbsp almond/peanut butter

1 tsp vanilla essence

Pinch of sea salt flakes

For the choc pots

12 oz soft silken tofu

4 oz vegan dark chocolate

2 tbsp coconut oil

Topping

Fresh fruit

Gooey caramel choc cups

These rich, chocolatey caramel cups are amazing! The magic ingredient is silken tofu, which makes them super-dreamy-creamy.

TO MAKE THE CARAMEL

Add the caramel ingredients to a food processor and blend until you get a super smooth paste. You may need to scrape down the sides a few times.

TO MAKE THE CHOC CUPS

1. Add the tofu to your caramel mix, and blend until very smooth and creamy.
2. Break up the chocolate and add to a saucepan with the coconut oil. Heat very gently on a low heat until melted. Don't overstir.
3. Add the chocolate to the mix in your food processor, and blend until very smooth.
4. Transfer into serving glasses or ramekins and chill in the fridge for an hour or until they're set.

INGREDIENTS
Serves 8-10

....

8-oz bar vegan chocolate, broken up

2 tbsp peanut or almond butter

1 tbsp maple syrup

Toppings

6 tbsp nuts of your choice—cashews, pistachios, flaked almonds, peanuts

2 tbsp seeds of your choice—sunflower, pumpkin, sesame

2 tbsp dried fruit of your choice—goji, cranberry, cherries

Super nutty peanut butter galaxy bark

Chocolate bark is really easy to make and tastes amazing. It also makes a great edible gift!

TO MAKE THE BARK

1. Add the nuts to a pan, heat to medium, and dry toast until lightly toasted—this is optional, but it adds to the flavor.

2. Now melt the chocolate in a microwave-safe bowl in 30-second increments, stirring after each one. But be careful and don't overdo it. The chocolate is done when it's about 90% melted—keep stirring off the heat and the pieces should completely dissolve. Alternately, you can melt it in a heatproof bowl set over a saucepan of gently simmering water.

3. Now stir in the peanut butter and maple syrup.

4. Pour the chocolate mixture onto the baking tray lined with greaseproof paper.

5. Top with the toasted nuts, seeds, and fruit.

6. Pop into the fridge until completely firm (this will take an hour or so). Remove and break into chunks.

Niki's tip
You can store in the freezer for when you fancy a chocolate treat, and eat it straight from there—cold but delicious.

For the cookies

3 very ripe bananas

1 tbsp peanut butter

1 tbsp vanilla essence

¾ cup white
self-rising flour

2 tbsp coconut oil

½ cup rolled oats

1 tsp baking powder

2 oz ground almonds

3 tbsp sesame seeds

2 oz vegan choc chips

For the "nice cream"

2 medium ripe bananas

3 tbsp peanut butter—
smooth or chunky

3 tbsp maple syrup

1 tsp vanilla syrup or
essence

Giant banana bread cookies & peanut butter banana "nice cream"

Do giant banana bread cookies sound good? They taste amazing, especially topped with the banana peanut butter "nice cream"—double peanut butter banana love.

TO MAKE THE COOKIES

1. Preheat your oven to 350°F.
2. Mix all the dry ingredients in a large bowl.
3. Melt the coconut oil in a saucepan on a low heat and then pour into a separate medium size bowl. Add in the bananas and mash up. Now add the maple syrup, vanilla essence, and peanut butter—mix to combine everything.
4. Add the wet ingredients to the dry and mix really well to combine everything. Stir in the choc chips.
5. Line a large baking tray with parchment paper then scoop up the mix into balls and pop them onto the lined baking tray. I made 4-5 large cookies.
6. Flatten the mix a bit with your hands.
7. Bake for around 18 minutes until slightly brown on the outside. Allow to cool.

TO MAKE THE BANANA "NICE CREAM"

1. The night before, peel, slice, and add the bananas to a freezer bag or tub and freeze.
2. Add the frozen bananas to a food processor or high-speed blender with the other ingredients. Blend until smooth and creamy.
3. Scoop out with an ice cream scoop or large spoon and top your banana bread cookies!

For the cake

1 ¼ cup plain flour

1 oz ground almonds

⅓ cup vegan brown sugar

2 oz cacao powder

2 tsp baking powder

1 tsp baking soda

½ tsp salt

1 ½ cups almond milk or plant-based milk of choice

½ cup light veg oil

1 tsp apple cider vinegar

1 tsp vanilla syrup or essence

For the topping

3 oz vegan butter/spread

2 tbsp Biscoff spread or peanut butter

2 tbsp cacao powder

1 tsp vanilla syrup or essence

Gooey chocolate cake with Biscoff frosting

I love chocolate cake—this one is richly chocolatey, soft, and gooey. It's a perfect celebration cake for a birthday or just a weekend treat.

TO MAKE THE CAKE

1. Preheat your oven to 350°F.
2. Line a high-sided medium size baking tray or dish with parchment paper.
3. In a large bowl, mix the dry ingredients well. Now add the wet ingredients and mix well to combine to a thick batter.
4. Spoon into the tray and smooth out to the sides.
5. Pop in the oven for 25–30 minutes—or just until the center is set and a toothpick inserted comes out with only a few moist crumbs.

TO MAKE THE TOPPING

1. Mix all the ingredients in a bowl to combine well.
2. Remove the cake from the oven and allow to cool before turning out and spreading the topping.

Niki's tip

Make sure you store in an airtight container to stop the cake from drying out.

INGREDIENTS

Makes one mug cake

For the cake

1 oz vegetable oil

¼ cup plant milk of your choice

⅓ cup self-raising flour

1 tsp baking powder

1 tbsp vegan brown sugar

1 tbsp maple syrup

½ tsp cinnamon

1 tsp vanilla essence

2 oz grated carrots

3 tbsp mixed dried fruits —sultanas or raisins

2 tbsp chopped nuts —walnuts, pecans, hazelnuts

Toppings

Plant-based yoghurt

Vegan cream cheese

Carrot cake mug cake

The magic of a mug cake: mix the ingredients, add to a mug, microwave, and *voilà!* a cake appears. The mix also works in the oven if you don't have a microwave. It's the same principle, just mix and bake—I would recommend doubling the mix for this option so you get 6 little cupcakes.

OPTION 1—MICROWAVE

1. Measure out the oil and plant-based milk and then add it to a mixing bowl.

2. Now grate the carrots, weigh them out, and add them along with the remaining ingredients to the bowl.

3. Mix to combine thoroughly and transfer to a large microwave-proof mug.

4. Cook on high power (850w) for about 2 minutes until risen, just set on the top and springy to the touch. Or on 750w for approx. 2 minutes 30 seconds.

5. Leave to stand for 1 minute. You can top and eat out of the mug or transfer to a plate to share.

OPTION 2—OVEN

1. Pre-heat your oven to 350°F.

2. Measure out the oil and plant-based milk and then add it to a mixing bowl.

3. Now grate the carrots, weigh them out, and add them along with the remaining ingredients to the bowl.

4. Mix to combine thoroughly, then spoon into three cupcake cases and transfer to your baking tray.

5. Bake for 20 minutes until cooked through, then remove from the oven and allow to cool.

Niki's tip

Have fun with the toppings—vegan cream cheese is delicious, or just dollop some yogurt on top.

8 oz medjool dates
pitted or dates soaked to
soften for a few hours

2 large ripe bananas
peeled

3 tbsp nut butter—
peanut/almond

1 tsp vanilla essence

1 tsp cinnamon

Pinch of sea salt flakes

1 tsp baking powder

3 oz ground almonds

1 ¾ cups porridge oats

3 tbsp chopped nuts—
hazelnuts, almonds, plus
a few more to top

4 tbsp vegan chocolate
chips or cacao nibs—
plus a few more to top

2 oz vegan chocolate,
broken up

Chopped nuts

Choc-dipped nutty choc chip oat cookies

These little nutty choc-dipped cookies are delish! They're healthy enough for breakfast (maybe minus the chocolate) but make a sweet little treat as well.

TO MAKE THE COOKIES

1. Preheat your oven to 350°F.
2. Pop the dates, banana, and nut butter into your food processor and blend to a smooth paste.
3. Next add in the vanilla, cinnamon, salt, and baking powder. Blend again for a minute.
4. Add in the oats and ground almonds and pulse so that everything is combined.
5. Now add in the choc chips and chopped nuts and pulse a couple of times to mix through.
6. Line a large baking tray with some parchment paper, then scoop up a tablespoon at a time and place on the baking tray. Continue until you have used all the mix.
7. Wet your hand a little and flatten the cookies. Top with more nuts and choc chips—press them in a little.
8. Bake for about 18 minutes, and allow to cool.

TO DIP THE COOKIES

1. Very gently melt the chocolate in a small pan. Only stir when the chocolate has melted.
2. One by one, coat one half in melted chocolate, then put them on a baking sheet.
3. Sprinkle with chopped nuts.
4. Allow the cookies to set in the fridge, then serve and enjoy!

Glossary

USEFUL TERMS

CRUELTY-FREE
Not tested on animals.

DAIRY-FREE
Contains no dairy products like cow's milk, cheese, butter, yogurt, or cream.

ETHICAL VEGANISM
Ethical vegans are those who don't just eat a plant-based diet, but also oppose the use of animals in any part of their life, including clothing, animal testing, and animal labor.

FLEXITARIANISM
A flexitarian is someone who still eats meat and dairy, but is trying to include more plant-based meals in their diet.

PESCETARIANISM
Vegetarians who also eat seafood are known as pescetarians.

PLANT-BASED
A plant-based diet consists of plants including vegetables, fruit, pulses, grains, nuts, and seeds. Not necessarily the same as vegan, as some plant products can cause cruelty to animals (see page 18).

VEGANISM
According to the Vegan Society, "a way of living which seeks to exclude, as far as is possible and practicable, all forms of exploitation of, and cruelty to, animals for food, clothing, or any other purpose."

VEGETARIANISM
The practice of avoiding any meat products, including red meat, poultry, and seafood. Most vegetarians still eat dairy products like cow's milk and cheese.

COOKING TECHNIQUES & INGREDIENTS

BAKING POWDER—A dry leavening agent, used to increase the volume and lighten the texture of baked goods

BEAT—To mix vigorously with a spoon, mixer, or spatula

BAKING SODA— A mixture of sodium and hydrogen carbonate. When it's mixed with acid (such as vinegar) it creates carbon dioxide which causes the mixture to expand before it's replaced with air.

BLEND—To make a liquid using a food processor or blender

BOIL—To heat liquid until it bubbles

CHOP—To cut something into small pieces

COMBINE—To mix ingredients together

DICE—To cut into small cubes

DISSOLVE—To melt or liquify something, usually into water

DRAIN—To remove excess liquid, using a sieve or colander

DRIZZLE—To pour slowly

FOLD—To fold something into a batter without stirring, i.e. choc chips into cake batter

GRATE—To shred into small pieces using a grater

GREASE—To rub oil or spread onto a baking tray or pan to stop sticking

HARISSA—Hot sauce or paste made from chili pepper, paprika, and oil

KNEAD—To fold and squash dough repeatedly, to make it more elastic

JUICE—To squeeze liquid out

LUKEWARM—Mildly warm, not hot

MINCE—To chop into extremely small pieces

PREHEAT—To turn on the oven so it can reach the correct temperature before cooking or baking

PULSE—Any food from the legume family, including peas, beans, chickpeas, soybeans, and lentils

PURÉE—To blend fruit or vegetables to a thick pulp

RINSE—To clean by washing under cold water

SEASON—To add salt and pepper to dishes to add flavor

SAUTÉ—To cook/fry in a pan with oil

SEITAN—Wheat gluten, used to make meat substitutes

SET—To leave food until it firms up

SIMMER—To heat liquid in a pan on a low heat, until small bubbles rise from it

SOY—A legume native to east Asia. The bean is used to make soy milk, tofu, soy sauce, and tempeh.

STIR FRY—To fry rapidly over a high heat, stirring constantly to prevent burning

TEMPEH—A soybean curd, chewier and denser than tofu

TOFU—A curd made of processed soybeans

TAHINI—Sesame seed paste

WHIP—To beat something to incorporate more air into it

WHISK—To mix vigorously with a whisk

ZEST—The grated skin of any citrus fruit

FURTHER READING & RESOURCES

VEGAN, ENVIRONMENTAL, AND ANIMAL RIGHTS ORGANIZATIONS

The Vegan Society	**www.vegansociety.com**
The Vegetarian Society	**www.vegsoc.org**
Extinction Rebellion	**rebellion.global**
Veganuary	**us.veganuary.com**
Surge	**www.surgeactivism.org**
NASA Climate Change	**climate.nasa.gov**

NEWS AND PUBLICATIONS

Plant Based News	**www.plantbasednews.org**
Vegnews	**www.vegnews.com**
Vegan Food and Living	**www.veganfoodandliving.com**
Raise Vegan	**www.raisevegan.com**
Live Kindly	**livekindly.co**
Vegan Life	**www.veganlifemag.com**

BOOKS

- *The China Study*, T. Colin Campbell
- *How Not To Die*, Dr. Michael Greger
- *Farmageddon*, Philip Lymbery
- *No One Is Too Small to Make a Difference*, Greta Thunberg
- *Should We All Be Vegan*, Molly Watson

TV & DOCUMENTARIES

- *Climate Change: The Facts*, (BBC) 2019
- *The Game Changers*, 2018
- *What the Health*, 2017
- *Cowspiracy*, 2014
- *Forks Over Knives*, 2011

Index